My Body

Why do I run?

Angela Royston

QED Publishing

A catalogue record for this book is
available from the British Library.

ISBN 978 1 84835 216 2

Printed and bound in China

Author Angela Royston
Consultant Terry Jennings
Project Editor Judith Millidge
Designer and Picture Researcher
Louise Downey

Publisher Steve Evans
Creative Director Zeta Davies
Managing Editor Amanda Askew

Picture credits

(t=top, b=bottom, l=left, r=right, c=centre, fc=front cover)
Corbis Christian Liewig 6, Hutchings Stock Photography
12, Gareth Brown 16–17, Sam Diephuis/zefa 18–19,
Emely/zefa 20
Getty Images Kaz Nanakubo 8, Tod Bigelow 13b,
Erik Dreyer 16t
Shutterstock JJ pixs 2lt, Jacek Chabraszewski 4, David
Davis 5t, Jacek Chabraszewski 5br, Losevsky Pavel 7b,
paparazzit 10, Gelpi 11l, phdpsx 11r, cen 13tl, Dole 13tc,
photobeps 13tr, Matka Wariatka 14b, Sinan Isakovic 15,
Serhiy Kyrychenko 17, Matt Antonino 18–19t, Leah-Anne
Thompson 19t, Tamara Kulikova 18t

Words in **bold** are explained
in the glossary on page 22.

Contents

Healthy exercise 4

Stronger muscles 6

Breathing 8

Stamina 10

Stronger bones 12

Moving your joints 14

Warming up 16

Ball play 18

Cooling down 20

Glossary 22

Notes for parents and teachers 23

Index 24

Healthy exercise

Brain · · · · ·

Heart · · ·

Running around is fun and it helps to make your body strong and healthy. Running exercises your muscles and bones. It also makes your heart and lungs work better.

Lungs · · ·

Hip bones

Leg muscles

Exercise makes you feel good. It helps your brain to work better, too.

4

Climbing and swinging are both great fun. They are also a good way to exercise.

Running is one kind of exercise. There are many others, including swimming and cycling.

Walking is good exercise, too. Walking to school is healthier than going by car.

5

Stronger muscles

You use your **muscles** to move. Muscles move your bones so that you can move the different parts of your body. The more you exercise, the stronger your muscles become.

This tennis player has large, strong arm muscles.

Muscles are made of bundles of strings, called muscle fibres. Exercising a muscle makes the fibres thicker and stronger. This makes your muscle bigger.

All muscles in your body, including arm muscles, are made of fibres.

Muscle fibres

Activity

Feel your muscles. Sit on the floor with your legs bent in front of you. Hold the back of your legs, then straighten them. Can you feel the leg muscles tightening?

7

Breathing

Air contains **oxygen**, which every part of your body needs. The harder your muscles work, the more oxygen they need. This makes you breathe deeper and faster.

Running exercises your lungs and heart, as well as your legs.

Your heart and lungs keep your body supplied with blood that contains oxygen.

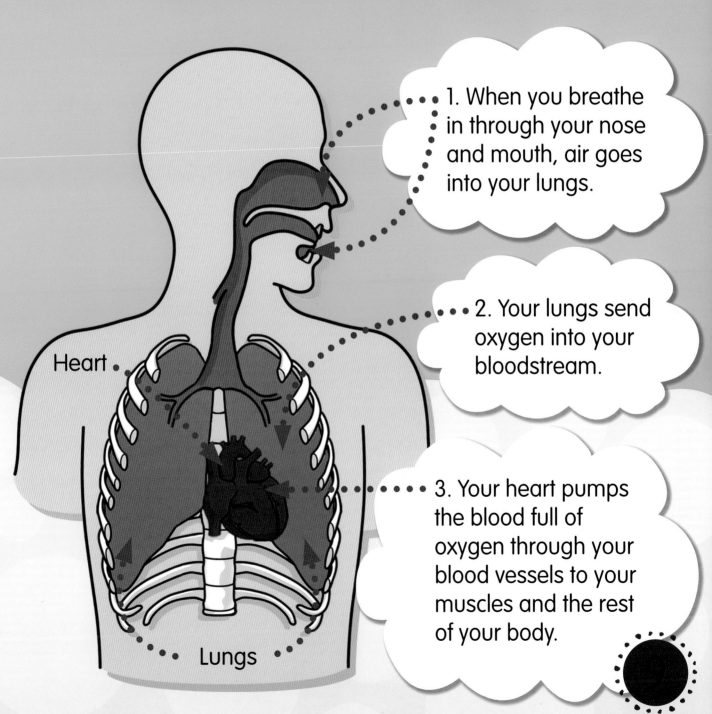

Heart

Lungs

1. When you breathe in through your nose and mouth, air goes into your lungs.

2. Your lungs send oxygen into your bloodstream.

3. Your heart pumps the blood full of oxygen through your blood vessels to your muscles and the rest of your body.

Stamina

Exercises that make you breathe faster help your heart and lungs to work better. The better they work, the longer you can keep going. This is called **stamina**.

This person has plenty of stamina. He can keep dancing without getting out of breath.

Your heart is a kind of muscle. Exercise makes it stronger. Exercises that make you breathe faster are called aerobic exercises. Running, swimming and dancing are different sorts of aerobic exercise.

Swimming is one kind of aerobic exercise.

Activity

Run on the spot, lifting your knees as high as you can. Keep going for as long as you can. Doing this every day will increase your stamina.

11

Stronger bones

Your bones are strong because they contain calcium. Some exercises help to make your bones stronger. For example, running puts extra force or weight on your leg bones. This makes them take in more calcium.

Skipping helps to make your leg bones stronger. This is because jumping up and down puts extra force on the bones.

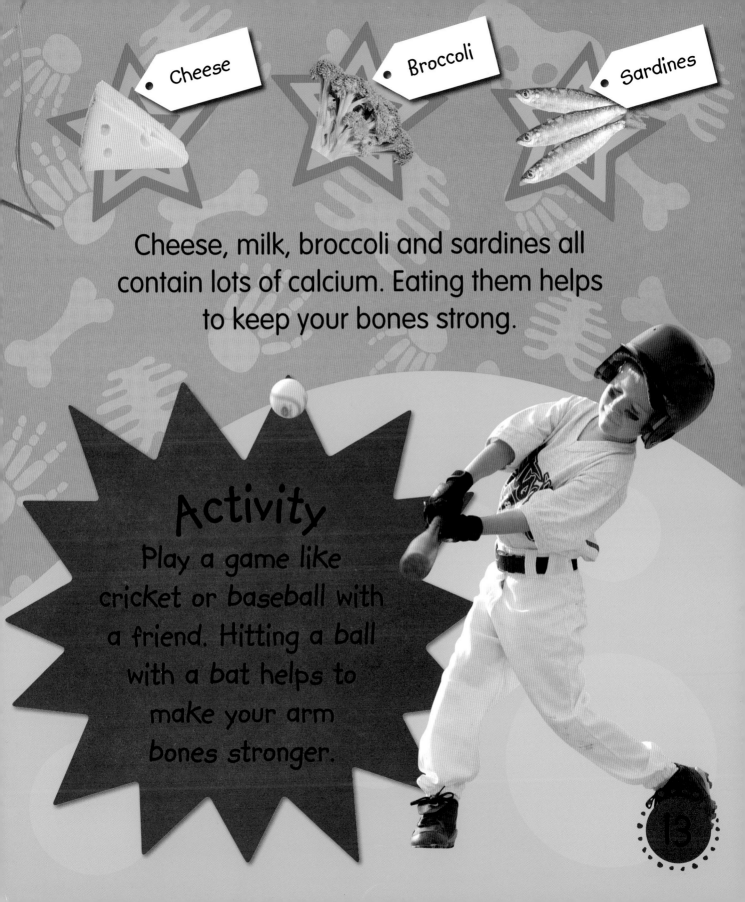

Cheese

Broccoli

Sardines

Cheese, milk, broccoli and sardines all contain lots of calcium. Eating them helps to keep your bones strong.

Activity

Play a game like cricket or baseball with a friend. Hitting a ball with a bat helps to make your arm bones stronger.

Moving your joints

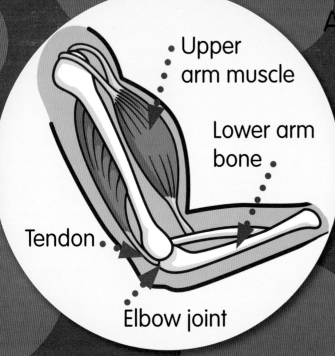

- Upper arm muscle
- Lower arm bone
- Tendon
- Elbow joint

A **joint** is where two bones meet. You can only move your bones at your joints. A tough strap of flesh called a **tendon** joins a muscle to the bone.

Tendons join the muscles in the upper arm to the bones in the lower arm. These muscles move your lower arm at the elbow.

Activity

Stretch your hip joints. Sit on the floor and cross your legs. Take one foot and put it on the other knee. Can you do the same with the other foot?

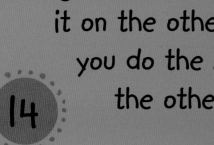

14

Some exercises stretch your muscles and tendons so that your joints move more easily. For example, swimming exercises your shoulder joints. Ballet dancing stretches your hip and ankle joints.

Shoulder

Hip

Ballet dancers who practise a lot have joints that move easily.

Ankle

15

Warming up

You need to warm up your muscles
before you do any energetic exercise.
You can warm up by walking and then
running gently.

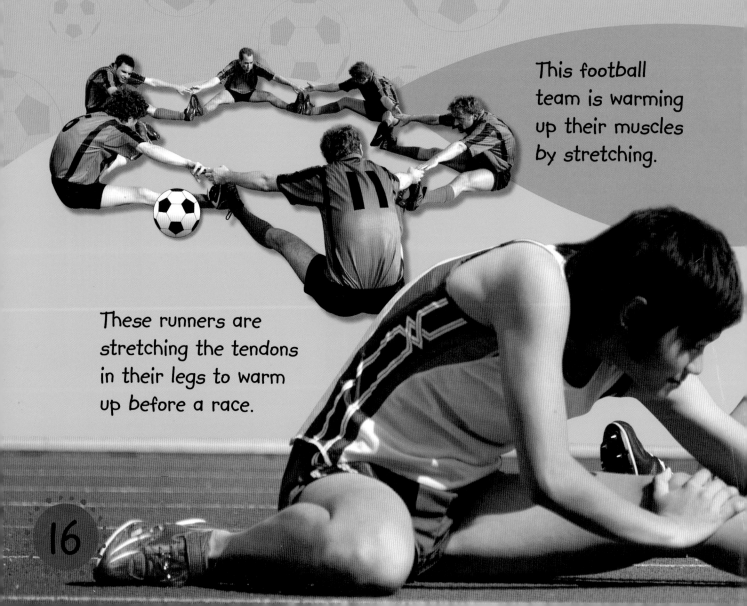

This football
team is warming
up their muscles
by stretching.

These runners are
stretching the tendons
in their legs to warm
up before a race.

16

The more you exercise, the fitter you become, but you should gradually increase the amount of exercise you do. A little bit more exercise each day will make your muscles stronger and increase your stamina.

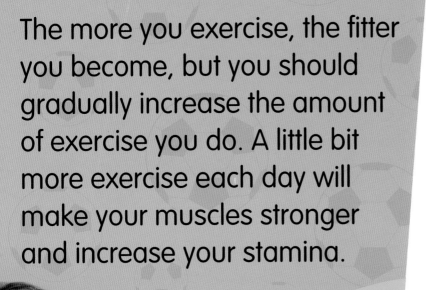

Activity

Try these warming-up exercises.

1. Stand on one leg and bend the other foot back to touch your bottom.

2. Keeping your legs straight, touch one foot and then the other foot.

17

Ball play

Juggling needs good hand-and-eye co-ordination.

Many games involve throwing and catching balls. You need good **co-ordination** to do these sports well. Co-ordination involves using your eyes and brain to time your movements correctly.

Your brain, eyes and muscles work together to help you head a ball.

Activity

Improve your ball skills!
Keep a football in the air.
You can use any part of
your body except your
hands and arms. How many
'keepie-uppies' can you do?

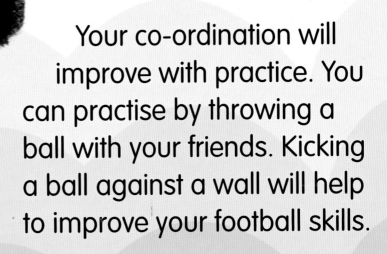

Your co-ordination will
improve with practice. You
can practise by throwing a
ball with your friends. Kicking
a ball against a wall will help
to improve your football skills.

19

Cooling down

It is important to allow your body to cool down gently after exercise. Cooling-down exercises help your muscles, heart and lungs to slow down before resting.

Having a rest after exercising gives your body a chance to recover.

Exercise can make you hot and sweaty. If the air is cold, put on a jumper, so that you do not cool down too fast.

Running around and sweating often makes you thirsty, so have a drink afterwards.

Activity

Marching on the spot is a good cooling-down activity. March slower and slower, and then stop.

Glossary

Co-ordination

The ability to make your muscles and senses work together at the right time. When you catch a ball, your eyes track the path of the ball. Your muscles then move your hands to catch it.

Joint

Where two bones meet and fit together. Most joints allow the bones to move in a particular way. Your knee lets your lower leg bend and straighten, and your shoulder joint allows you to circle your arm.

Muscles

Parts of the body that you use to move. Some muscles move your bones, but others do not. For example, muscles in your face move your cheeks. Your tongue and heart are also muscles.

Oxygen

One of the gases in the air. Every part of your body uses oxygen to work. Blood picks up oxygen from the air you breathe into your lungs. Your heart then pumps the blood to every part of your body.

Stamina

The ability to keep going without running out of breath when you are exercising. If you have plenty of stamina, your lungs can take in a lot of air without you having to breathe very fast, and your heart can pump a lot of blood around your body without having to beat very fast.

Tendon

A tough strap that joins a muscle to the bone it moves. A tendon stretches across a joint so that it can make a bone move at that joint.

Notes for parents and teachers

1. Children with heart or breathing problems should be carefully supervised and should not be allowed to over-exert themselves.

2. Encourage children to be involved in keeping themselves healthy. Talk to them about how exercise is good for their health, because it makes their muscles and bones stronger, and makes their heart and lungs work better. Explain that exercise also makes people feel good.

3. Children are most likely to exercise if they enjoy it. Health experts recommend that all children should exercise for at least an hour a day. This does not have to be all at once, and is often best broken down into periods of 15 minutes.

4. If possible, walk or cycle to school, instead of driving by car. Encourage children to exercise during breaks at school. There are many ways that children can exercise at playtime, including playing on the climbing frame, running around playing 'tag' and playing ball games.

5. Give children plenty of opportunity to take part in sports and activities they enjoy, such as playing football, swimming and dancing. Set an example by joining in, too. Most children enjoy practising football or throwing a Frisbee with an adult.

6. A trip to a local park where they can play on swings, roundabouts and other equipment is both fun and healthy.

Index

ball games 13, 18–19
blood 9, 22
bones 4, 6, 12–13, 14, 22
brain 4, 18
breathing 8–9, 10, 11, 22

calcium 12, 13
cooling down 20–21
co-ordination 18, 19, 22
cycling 5

dancing 10, 11, 15
drink 21

exercise 4–5, 6, 7, 8, 10,
    11, 12, 15, 16, 17,
    20, 21
eyes 18, 22

heart 4, 8, 9, 10, 11, 20, 22

joints 14–15, 22

lungs 4, 8, 9, 10, 20, 22

muscles 4, 6–7, 8, 9, 14,
    15, 16, 17, 20, 22

oxygen 8, 9, 22

running 4, 5, 8, 11, 12, 16

skipping 12
stamina 10–11, 17, 22
stretching 14, 16
sweating 21
swimming 5, 11, 15

tendons 14, 15, 16, 22

walking 5, 16
warming up 16–17